I0068174

The START LEAN and MEAN™ Series

NEW
Business
Launch
GUIDE

NIURKA CASTANEDA

Published by
Niurka Castaneda

ISBN: 978-1-7364815-9-2 (Softcover)
ISBN: 978-1-7364815-8-5 (Ebook)

Cover and Interior: Gary A. Rosenberg • www.thebookcouple.com

PROLOGUE

The New Business Launch Guide presents a step-by-step action plan, delivered in easy bites, that makes the whole process of launching your business process easy and manageable. This way, you can focus on building your business instead of feeling overwhelmed by all the things that need to be taken care of when you start a new business.

Hey there!

This guide will give you insight into what it takes to create and launch your new business.

- Start slow; take it one day at a time, one step at a time.

- The key is to just **START**, but start **Lean and Mean**, and always remember that: "**Cash is King**."

Learn to be conservative with your funds from the beginning. Have at least a fundamental knowledge of what is needed before you hire out and learn your business numbers.

Take control of your business from the start by learning how to leverage your expenses against your profit by going beyond the traditional way of calculating your profit.

Sales – Expenses = Profit *vs.*

Sales – Profit = Expenses

FOCUS **ON THE BASICS**

Starting a business is pretty simple . . . but that doesn't mean it's easy. Don't get distracted by the shiny objects, instead, work on creating the foundation of your business really well. That is what successful entrepreneurs do. Get back to the basics.

New Business Launch Checklist

	N/A	Not Done	Done
1. Business name, availability and name search			
a. Choose a Name			
b. Verify Name Availability			
c. Secure the Domain Name			
2. Business Address and Corporate Structure			
a. Determine Your Business Address			
b. Decide on a Corporate Structure			
3. Registration and EIN			
a. Register Your Business			
b. Obtain a EIN Number			
Update your state registration			
Elect to be taxed as a S Corp (LLC only)			
4. Business Bank Account and Credit Card			
a. Open a Business Bank Account			
b. Open a Business Credit Card			

	N/A	Not Done	Done
5. DUNs Number			
a. Apply for a DUNs Number			
6. Register with SBA & SAM			
a. Apply for the Certifications that Apply to your Business			
Apply online with SBA			
8(a) Business Development			
Hubzone			
Self Certify: SAM.gov			
Service-Disabled Veteran Owned Small Business			
Economically Disadvantaged Woman Owned Small Business			
Woman Owned Small Business			
Small Disadvantaged Owned Business			

YOUR BUSINESS
Where to Start?

Ideas... ideas are great!!! As a new entrepreneur, you will not run out of them in the beginning, but it is also important to do your research with lots of planning. A business takes a lot of work, so make sure it is something that you are passionate about.

> *"I'm convinced that about half of what separates the successful entrepreneurs from the non-successful ones is pure perseverance.... Unless you have a lot of passion about this, you're not going to survive. You're going to give it up. So you've got to have an idea or a problem or a wrong that you want to right that you're passionate about; otherwise, you're not going to have the perseverance to stick it through."*
>
> *—Steve Jobs*

Sometimes as entrepreneurs we underestimate the work that is involved in setting up a business. While every company is unique in its own way, there are some basic business fundamentals that all companies share.

Disclosure: It is recommended that you seek the advice of a CPA for taxes purposes and the advice of an attorney for legal purposes.

Where do you start?

Start by choosing a NAME for your new Business. It will help you visualize it.

1. CHOOSE A NAME

Choosing a business name, not just any name but the right name, is a key consideration for your business. It will be the first impression of your company that your customer will see. It can be a powerful tool that can make a big impact on your business. Take your time, but keep it legal, simple, and not too restrictive. Choose a name that has not been trademarked, that your business can grow with it. Imagine your brand and business name 10, 20, or 100 years in the future. It should hint what your brand is and what your business does.

Make sure you are happy with the name selected. If later on you are still not satisfied with it, you could decide to change it for branding purposes to attract new customers or to modernized it.

Still not sure?

Have you heard of a company called *GOOGLE*? Do you know that their original name was "BackRub"? It was changed to Google in 1998 by its founders, and it is an intentional misspelling of the mathematical term 'googol' that represents the number one (1) followed by hundred zeros.

➤ Make it easy to remember:
  • Do not be afraid to try out names and made up

words, but try to choose a name that is short, memorable, suggestive, emotional, and that rolls off the tongue easily.

- Use imagery in your name if possible as people will remember it more easily than words and random letters.

For example: The heart symbol has been associated with love and romance since the 13th century, and some brands use to replace the word "Love" and its foreign translations like "Amor" and "Amour."

- Can you create a theme out of it?

For example: Latitude Margaritaville retirement communities use street names that are fun, relatable, and theme-based like *Castaway Court* and *Flip Flop Lane.* Their dog park is named *Barkaritaville*!

Note: Having a name with a good theme could help create unlimited branding opportunities in the future.

- Does your business name help you create an emotion?

Customers would be attracted to it on an emotional level if it resonates with them.

According to Forrester Research, "50% of every buying decision is driven by emotion. Not only do we buy things that make us feel good, but we are also inclined to buy things with names that make us feel good."

Does it seem that all the good names are already taken?

What about *NETFLIX*? or Kodak, Lexus, Spotify...? Those names all have something in common: They sounded a little odd or quirky at first—and meaning-less—but soon they soon became very accepted and powerful brand names.

Things to remember when choosing a name for your business

➤ Remember that trademarked names are not legal to use and would be difficult to market due to trademark and copyright laws.

➤ Stay away, if possible, from *special symbols, numbers, or hyphens* in the name or anything else that would make it hard to spell your business name. Do not confuse people; it will frustrate them, and you don't want your customers to have that experience about your brand. This could lead to misspelling of the name.

"If you have to spell it over the phone, you've lost."

—Jason Calacanis

(Serial entrepreneur and angel investor behind tech giants like Uber, the Launch Festival, and This Week in Startups)

➤ *Do NOT make it too long, complicated, or make it look like a typo* because there would be more potential for people to misspell it when searching, and you could lose internet traffic to your competitors...Think of it from your potential clients' point of view.

➤ Does it have a personality? Let your name help you get noticed.

Running Low on Ideas?

Use a domain name generator tool to spark ideas. Some that I particular like are NameMesh.com, naminum.com, Shopify Business Name Generator, and VisualThesaurus.com that help you get you a visual around a keyword; eatmywords.com offers a free test that can help you test your chosen brand name. They are user-friendly. Try to think of at least three potential alternatives names in case the first two are not available.

2. VERIFY NAME AVAILABILITY

Now that you have a name in mind, you need to make sure is still available in the state where you want to incorporate. Use an original name and not a copycat word. Let your name help you stand out from the competition.

Start by searching if your business name is available:

- Start by doing a simple internet search
- Check your state for name availability:

    Florida: sunbiz.org/search.html

    North Carolina: sosnc.gov/divisions/
        business_registration

- Do a search at USPTO.gov to make sure it has not been trademarked already.

Use a domain name generator like namemesh.com to look at potential domain names and generate ideas. Pay attention to the ".com" column in particular, for the reason that most people automatically search *for .com. (the "big three and most used suffixes" are* .com, .net and .org). ".COM" is the most recognized and memorable domain due to its history, while people might struggle to remember other generic domain suffixes. There are hundreds of variations of domain suffixes like ".biz," ".camera," ".best," ".shop"—and they are often used for spam!

For that reason, they potentially have an immediate SEO penalty or a lack of trust. In other words, you might lose website traffic as a result. Google, the number one search engine , knows the world prefers .com which means it will help your SEO (Search Engine Optimization) and cost you less money spend for advertising. However because ".com" is so popular, it might be difficult to find a name you like, so the next best options are ".org" (mostly used for a non-profit foundation), ".net" or location-specific domain suffix.

3. CHECK TO SEE IF YOUR BUSINESS NAME IS TRADEMARKED

Make sure that your business name is not under copyright or trademarked, you'll want to use TESS (Trademark Electronic Search System).

➤ A trademark can be or include:

- a name
- a symbol ("I ♥ New York" motto)
- a logo
- a color
- a sound
- a three-dimensional shape

4. SECURE THE DOMAIN NAME

Buying a domain is pretty simple; there are several sites that sells domain names; most website hosts like Shopify, Wix, and Google also sell their own. One of the most popular and known domain providers is godaddy.com, but you also can use namesh.com.

Whomever you decide to use, the important thing would be to remember to purchase the domain for at least two years as it helps you rank better with Google; if a domain is close to expiring, Google may choose to ignore it.

You also want to include the domain and privacy option for your purchases for security purposes. Protect your assets!

Finally, when you have found a name that you are happy with and you are ready to move forward, it is time to secure your domain name before somebody else snatches it. They are relatively cheap, so don't hold off.

Note: You might want to set it up atomically to renew because if your domain expires for even a day, the original price would go up astronomically. There are businesses out-there where all they do is buy expired domains, most likely to sell at premium rates. Your own domain name may cost you $2,000.00+ to acquire. Your domain name must be powerful enough to stand out on its own. It is a visual asset of your business and brand that would represent your business, and it could generate traffic on is own. It will also increase in value with time.

5. DETERMINE YOUR BUSINESS ADDRESS

Before you register your new business with your state of choice, you would need to decide and gather some information, such as the business address you will use for legal considerations and customer perception.

The answer to this question is pretty simple if you have a brick-and-mortar business. However, if you have a home or online business, and you do not want to use your home address as your publicly listed business address for privacy and security issues.

Fortunately, you have some options:

➤ You can choose not to list your address at all in your marketing material and website. However, consider customer perception of not offering an address. It could result in loss of trust and credibility and damage your professional image.

➤ **USPS's Enhanced Business PO Box:** Allows you to use the street address of your local post office where your PO Box is located, followed by the number sign (#), or you can use the more traditional PO Box address instead.

➤ **Mailbox services:** Much like USPS, this service is where you rent a mailbox at places like the UPS Store or Mail Boxes, Etc.; you can use the UPS Store's street address as your physical address and your mailbox number as a suite or apartment number.

➤ **Virtual Office Space:** Virtual office spaces or business addresses are places where they provide you with a professional-looking mailing address and other additional features and facilities, such as receptionist services and meeting spaces that can be rented when you need them.

➤ **Co-working space:** Similar to virtual office space, they provide you with a professional mailing address to use for your business. and meeting and conference rooms you can use as well. They also offer you a physical space to actually work in, along with the use of shared resources, such as Wi-Fi.

Note: A physical address is legally required for your business as a limited liability company (LLC), as a corporation, as a limited partnership, or as a limited liability partnership, where you will need to have a registered agent address in the state in which you have registered to do business. PO Box addresses cannot legally be used as a registered agent's address. A member of the LLC can serve as the registered agent for the business.

However, if you do not want your home address listed in public documents as the address of your registered agent, you will need to appoint a third-party to serve as your registered agent. The third-party can be an individual, such as an attorney, or it can be a company whose business offers registered agent services.

6. DECIDE ON A CORPORATE STRUCTURE

Should you incorporate, and, if so, what kind of corporation should you choose? There are several corporate
structures you can choose.

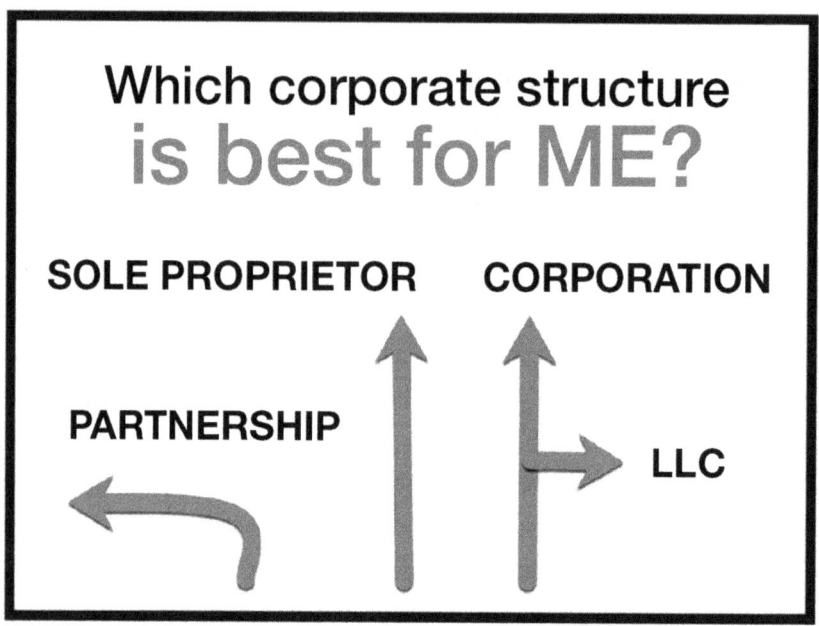

Carefully consider the pros and cons of different forms
of business organization that fit the needs of your small
business and the different ways these organizations can
be taxed. It is always a good idea to consult a CPA or an
attorney. They both might have different opinions. One
may analyze it from a legal perspective, and the other
from a taxation point of view. Keep in mind: Incorporating
under the incorrect structure could have severe financial
ramifications.

➤ **Sole proprietorship**

(the simplest of all the entities but with the most risk)

- A sole proprietorship can be formed instantly, easily, and inexpensively.

- In order to create a sole proprietorship, no state filling is required.

- Pass-through entities for tax purposes general partnership.

- There are no annual reports to file, nor fees to pay to the state, and no required annual meetings.

- The type of business that you start will determine what kind of business licenses and permits you would need.

- Unless you file a *DBA (doing business as),* your business name will be your personal name.

- Most financial institutions would require sole proprietors to have a DBA name in order to open a bank account.

- As a sole proprietor, you would be personally liable for any debts incurred by the business. Business creditors can go after a sole proprietor's personal assets like their home, car, and other personal property to satisfy debts.

➤ **Limited partnership**

- Pass-through entities for tax purposes general partnership.

➤ Partnership

- Pass-through entities for tax purposes general partnership.

➤ Limited liability company (LLC)

- Being taxed like an S-corporation is chosen the least by small business owners; it is an option that can actually provide a tax saving, particularly if the LLC has an active trade or business and the payroll taxes on the owner or owners are high.

- Provides limited liability protection to business owners, and they would not be typically held personally responsible for any business debts and liabilities. The amount of liability is limited to the amount of ownership or investment in the LLC.

- Unless C corporation tax treatment is elected, LLC's avoid double taxation by receiving pass-through of income to owners.

- All the net earnings of a LLC will pass through to the business owners in the form of self-employment income subject to 15.3% SECA tax (self-employment tax for Social Security and Medicare)

- A single member LLC is considered a "disregarded entity," meaning all the profits and income is subject to income and self-employment tax.

Note: Self-employment tax is 15.3% (12.4% for social security, 2.9% for medicare). Your ordinary income tax rate will depend on where you fall on the tax bracket. You can read more online.

➤ C Corporation

- Double taxation

- Usually the most common corporation type.

- Provides limited liability protection to owners (called shareholders), which means owners are typically not personally responsible for business debts and liabilities.

- It can have an unlimited number of individual share-holders. (Venture capitalists prefer it when providing funding to a business)

- It could retain earnings for reasonable business needs instead of distributing them to shareholders. Must comply with the accumulated earnings tax provisions.

- Easy transfer of ownership.

- Owners take reasonable salaries.

- Required to adopt corporate by-laws.

- Must hold an initial meeting of directors and shareholders.

- Must issue shares of stock to owners.

➤ S Corporation

- Pass-through entities for tax purposes general partnership.

- The business entity must be formed in the United States.

- S Corp cannot have more than 100 owners. They can be only individuals, and US residents can own interests.

- Only one class of owners is allowed, and they cannot be preferred shareholders or members.

- An entity taxed as a S corporation, where the owner works for the corporation and is considered an employee. Only the wages paid to its owner and/or employees are earned income that would be subject to FICA tax for Social Security and Medicare.

- The remaining net earnings can be distributed to you and other owners as passive dividend income, not subject to SECA tax.

- Use Form 2553 to make the special election with the IRS.

➤ Registering a DBA (Optional)

Once incorporated, you can also choose to do business under another name, also called a "Fictitious Business Name" (FBN) or "Doing Business As" name (DBA), which is different from the official legal name of your corporation. It must be registered with the Secretary of State or other entity that governs business formation in your state.

If your business operates in multiple states, your company's fictitious name must be registered in any state where you have a presence. Registering your "Fictitious Business Name" (FBN) or "Doing Business As" name (DBA) ensures that no one else is doing business under your name or your business name in the county.

Here are some examples of why you would use a DBA:

- If you are incorporating in multiple states under the same name, and you want your business name to include specific locations.
- The products and services you provide as a business have changed.

Note: Prepare ads in the newspaper that state your intention to do business under your "Doing Business As" name (DBA); keep a copy of the article for your records. Some states do not allow a "Fictitious Business Name" (FBN) or "Doing Business As" name (DBA). Research your state here.

➤ **Elect to be taxed as a S Corp (LLC only) (optional)**

If you decide to form a LLC to own and operate your business, you can choose how your LLC is to be taxed. A LLC can be taxed like a sole proprietorship, a partnership, a C corporation, or an S corporation. You can benefit from the combined features of using a LLC to own and operate your small business and then have it taxed like an S corporation.

7. REGISTER YOUR BUSINESS

A business name needs to be checked for availability within your chosen state prior to registering your business and filling your Articles of Incorporation.

➤ **What would you need?**

- **Corporate name:** Your corporate name must include your desired name, a corporate identifier like: "Corporation, Incorporated, Company," or an abbreviation such as "Inc."

- **Business purpose**

  Ask yourself these questions:

  —Why are you incorporating your company?

  —What are you going to do or what kind of service are you going to provide?

  There are two types of business purpose clauses:

  1. General: Some states accept an "all lawful business" clause to explain your business purpose.

  2. Specific: Some states require a specific explanation of the products and/or services your business will provide.

- **Registered agent:**

  The registered agent receives important legal and tax documents for the corporation, must have a physical address (no PO Boxes) in the state in which you are incorporating, and needs to be available during normal business hours.

- Number of authorized shares of stock:

  Corporations must outline the number of shares of stock they wish to authorize.

- Share par value:

  Common par values used are $0.01, $1.00, or no par.

- Legal address of the company: (some states require it)

  State filing costs for forming a LLC or corporation can vary from state to state. You can use this filing fee tool here to compare state fees before you start your business. There are several companies or attorneys that can help you incorporate. A great site that can walk you through the process of starting a LLC is LLC University.

  Some of them are Legal Zoom, IncFile

  Disclosure: *It is recommended that you seek the advice of a CPA for tax purposes and the advice of an attorney for legal purposes.*

8. OBTAIN AN EIN NUMBER

The EIN, or Employer Identification Number, is a 9-digit tax ID number issued by the Internal Revenue Service. It is used for identifying business entities.

It is required by the federal government for C corporations, partnerships, trusts, estates, and LLCs. Sole properties can also file for an EIN number

Use form SS-4 to apply (at not cost); you can request it directly at the <u>IRS</u> site.

Note: Don't forget to update your state registration with your new EIN number.

9. OPEN A BUSINESS BANK ACCOUNT

Even if you are 100% the owner of the business.

If you commingle personal and business expenses, you could lose all the legal protection that the entity structure, the LLC, or Corporation provided you in the first place. That means all your personal assets are at risk if the business is involved in a lawsuit or debtors need to collect assets.

The IRS can choose to revoke your business's S selection because you did not treat it as a separate entity, and you can end up owing additional taxes and penalties.

A simple way to avoid this is:

- Open a business account, and keep it separate from your personal account, making it easier for you to manage your business as your personal expenses don't mingle with your business expenses.
  - Choose the bank that will offer the best services that fit your small business, like lower business banking fees or banks that specialize in your industry.

—If you need to fund your business from your personal account, deposit it in your business account and track it in your budget sheet, either as a contribution or investment.

When you need to distribute funds to either collect the profit or pay yourself a wage or salary:

—Record the transaction as a business distribution (like a dividend from your business).

—If you pay yourself a salary, make sure to collect and pay any payroll taxes owed to the state where your business is registered.

To open an account you will need, at minimum:

- An EIN number (get one via the IRS for free)
- Social Security number (if you're a sole proprietor)
- Proof of incorporation (for business structures like LLCs)

IRS Factors in Determining Business vs. Hobby

➤ Do you look and act like a business?

➤ What is your relevant experience?

➤ How much time and effort do you invest?

➤ What is our history and track record?

➤ What are your total business assets?

- A business license or business name filing paperwork

10. OPEN A BUSINESS CREDIT CARD

In the beginning stages of your new business, keeping cash flow positive might be difficult, so having a business credit card to help you with the bills through the month is a good idea. Get a credit card to charge your daily and business expenses, but make sure you pay off your credit cards balance every month. *You CANNOT carry a balance on a business credit card.*

This strategy would also help you build your credit score as long as you pay your debts on time, every time. It is not to be used for overspending or for getting into debt. Always be strategic and intentional in the way you conduct business and handle money. Make sure to have cards that are going to be used for your personal purchases and a separate card for business purchases. NEVER, ever, co-mingle funds!!!

> # NEVER, EVER,
> ## CO-MINGLE FUNDS!
> # DON'T DO IT!

Pick up the credit card that offers you the best deal overall. Some questions to ask when considering credit cards are:

❐ How much does it cost to open an account?

❐ What is the annual fee?

❐ When does the introductory offer end?

❐ What is the interest rate?

❐ Are there late fees or other penalties?

❐ Does the card offer rewards?

❐ Do they offer miles?

❐ How quickly will you earn rewards, how much are they worth, and do they expire?

❐ Do they have foreign transaction fees?

❐ What is your credit limit? How often can you apply for an increase?

Note: Call your credit card companies (personal and business alike) yearly and ask them to increase you credit limit at a lower APR percentage.

➤ Some questions to ask:

• What is the lowest rate that they offer?

• Can you get it?

• Can you increase your credit limit?

Note: Pay attention to your credit score. You are entitled to receive your credit score for free from the three major credit reporting agencies every 12 months.

Get your free reports here: annualcreditreport.com

You can also use a compilation service for free such as creditkarma.com.

If you want a deeper look at your score and what it means, you can use myfico.com, but you would have to pay a fee.

Note: Keep track of your finances and maintain a budget (weekly, monthly, and yearly) Use an accounting software like Quickbooks or Mint.

11. RESEARCH A BUSINESS LICENSE REQUIREMENT

Does your kind of business or industry require a license?

Conduct a simple Google search to find out the license requirements for your business industry by your city, county, and state. Check with your local chamber of commerce.

12. OBTAIN INSURANCE

Would your kind of business and industry require you to have insurance for your overall business? Are you going to self-insure?

➤ Professional liability insurance:

- Protects business assets from claims that might result from your advice, expertise, or any professional services you provide.

- Protects you in cases of faulty service, errors, or failure to provide a service altogether (considered an omission). If someone felt you gave them "bad" advice, this insurance would cover you!

➤ General liability insurance:

- Protects small-business owners from claims of injury, property damage, and negligence related to business activities. The indemnity provided by a general liability insurance policy helps you cover the costs associated with a possible legal defense.

- If you see clients in person at your home, you might not be covered by your homeowner's policy; even if you see clients at your office, it's best to look into this if you meet with clients in person, regardless of location.

➤ Errors and omissions insurance:

- Your policy should include "Errors and omissions" insurance.

  Note: While you can choose to self-insure, make sure to weigh the pros and cons of that approach, especially if you are dealing directly with customers. Call your local insurance agent to find out available rates.

13. OBTAIN A DUNS NUMBER

The DUNS number or Data Universal Numbering System is a unique nine-digit identification number provided by the company Dun & Bradstreet. They assign DUNS numbers for each physical location of a business. Beware of scams or fraudulent organizations or websites soliciting a fee because registering for a DUNS number is free. (Get one via the Dun & Bradstreet website at dnb.com for free.)

What is a DUNS number used for?

DUNS numbers are often referenced by lenders, creditors, vendors, or potential partners as a business credit file to evaluate and identify a business for financial and readability health. It provides credibility to your company. Once assigned, the number does not change throughout the life of your business. It compares to a social security number for your business. It is the first step for having your business establish credit.

The federal government requires that anyone applying for federal grants or government contracts has a DUNS number. *Make sure to mention this purpose, and your application will get fast-tracked when applying.*

Upon registering, you will receive a copy of your PAYDEX score, similar to your personal credit FICO score that represents your business credit worthiness.

The score ranges from 0 to 100:

0 to 49 indicates a significant amount of risk

50 to 79 indicates a moderate risk

80 to 100 indicates a low risk.

You will need the following information to apply:

- Business name
- Business address
- Phone number
- Business owner's name
- Year founded
- Legal business's structure
- Number of employees

NOTE: The DUNS Number will be replaced in a future, to-be-determined date by the Unique Entity Identifier (UEI) requested in and assigned by the System for Award Management (SAM.gov). To learn more about SAM's rollout of the UEI, please visit gsa.gov/entityid

14. REGISTER WITH "SAM" (optional)

Registering with the System for Award Management (SAM) is required for your organization to be able to apply for federal grants, as well for contractors prior to being awarded a contract according to the Federal Acquisition Regulation (subpart 4.11). Contact the SAM Customer Assistance Center toll free at 1-888-227-2423.

What would you need?

- SAM will require a notarized letter submitted to them before they activate your entity registration.
- You would also need to designate an EBiz POC.
- Your DUNS Number
- Your EIN Number
- Your Electronic Funds Transfer (EFT) Information

- Your CAGE or NCAGE Number, if you already have one. If you do not have one, you can request one here, or you will be automatically assigned one by SAM

- Your NAICS codes; at least one NAICS code has to be associated with your business as its primary, but you can include as many as are applicable to you.

- SAM will verify and certify veteran-owned businesses.

Why should you certify?

Simple: The federal government wants to do business with your small business, and **THEY BUY EVERYTHING**!!!

References

https://www.legalzoom.com/articles/do-you-need-a-physical-address-for-your-business

https://www.grants.gov/web/grants/applicants/organization-registration/step-2-register-with-sam.html

https://www.bizfilings.com/toolkit/research-topics/incorporating-your-business/what-are-articles-of-incorporation

https://www.gsa.gov/about-us/organization/federal-acquisition-service/office-of-systems-management/integrated-award-environment-iae/iae-information-kit/unique-entity-identifier-update

https://dos.myflorida.com/sunbiz/start-business/corporate-structure/

https://www.bizfilings.com/toolkit/research-topics/managing-your-taxes/federal-taxes/llc-electing-s-corp-statusthe-best-of-both-worlds

https://www.bizfilings.com/starting-your-business/business-types/c-corporation

https://dos.myflorida.com/sunbiz/start-business/corporate-structure

https://www.incfile.com/fictitious-business-or-trade-name/

http://www.irs.gov/Businesses/Small-Businesses-&-Self-Employed/Apply-for-an-Employer-Identification-Number-(EIN)-Online

https://www.nerdwallet.com/article/taxes/federal-income-tax-brackets

https://smallgovcon.com/five-things/five-things-you-should-know-registering-in-sam-gov/

https://eportal.nspa.nato.int/AC135Public/CageTool/home

https://www.freshbooks.com/hub/accounting/set-up-business-bank-account

usps.com

https://www.forbes.com/sites/allbusiness/2016/10/23/12-tips-for-naming-your-startup-business/?sh=a5cddd3904e3

https://www.allbusiness.com/99-inspirational-quotes-for-entrepreneurs-18398-1.html/

https://companieshouse.blog.gov.uk/2019/02/14/symbols-and-characters-in-a-company-name/

The Author

©C. Sanchez

NIURKA CASTANEDA is a veteran entrepreneur and the founder, director, and host of Amor Umbrella TV and Founders Time Podcast. She is the mom of two incredible kids, and loves to write, travel, and take pictures.

Visit www.niurkacastaneda.com